To Rita and David
with fond memories
of Guernsey

Love from Carol & Nick

Spirit of Guernsey

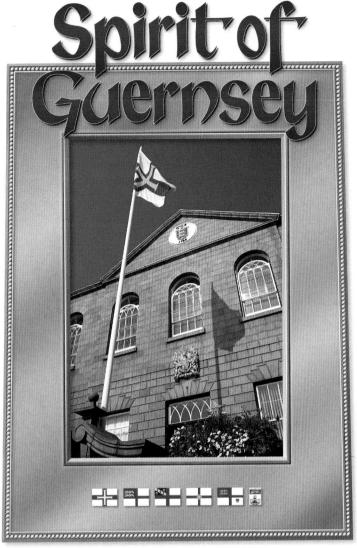

A PHOTOGRAPHIC PROFILE
OF THE BAILIWICK OF GUERNSEY
INCLUDING SARK, HERM, ALDERNEY, BRECQHOU AND JETHOU

Photography by	**Michael Thompson** **Miles Cowsill**
Written by	**Peter Davies** **and (Alderney) Ilona Soane-Sands**
Edited by	**Trevor Barrett**
Designed by	**Tracey Harding**
Published by	**Lily Publications Ltd** **PO Box 33 Ramsey** **Isle of Man IM99 4LP**
Telephone	**01624 898446**
ISBN	**1 899602 17 8**
First published	**October 2003**

Lily Publications
Limited

St Peter Port harbour is at the centre of island life. It is here that produce is landed and exported, the ferries travel back and forth between Guernsey, Jersey, England and France, the fishing fleet has its haven and the Guernseyman indulges his love of boating

When Guernsey wanted to mark the **50th anniversary** of its **Liberation** it was decided that an obelisk was the thing.

This imaginative work by local artist Eric Snell comprises a low wall on which the events of Liberation Day are marked and as the sun passes over on 9 May the shadow cast by the obelisk meets each event at the appropriate time. At least, that is what happened on 9 May 1995.

The Liberation Memorial is now widely used by lunchtime sunbathers, skate-boarders and people waiting for the ferry to Herm.

I welcome the publication of this new book of photographs of the very special islands of the Bailiwick of Guernsey.

Whilst I hope that those who open its pages will derive pleasure from it for a great many years, it is perhaps fitting that it is being published on the eve of 2004, a date which will not mean a great deal to many people, including some of those in these islands. We will then be celebrating the 800th anniversary of the loss of continental Normandy to the Crown of England. This event, perhaps above all others, provided the opportunity for the Bailiwick to develop its own character over the centuries. More important, this separation from both Normandy and England enabled us to develop our own institutions and our own system of law in a way best suited for, what remain today very small self-governing communities. The helpful text which accompanies the photographs endeavours to explain how we come to be as we are and it is paramount that people in future generations understand this and more crucially identify those aspects of our system of government and way of life which are so important to preserve.

A few years ago the people of Guernsey generously subscribed to a new lifeboat, which was then appropriately named 'Spirit of Guernsey'. I hope that the spirit of Guernsey remains one of independence and also one of generosity.

Sir de Vic G Carey
Bailiff and President of the States of Guernsey

Guernsey Maritime Map courtesy of UK Hydrographic Office

Location, location, location

Guernsey is located nearer to France than it is to England. That is the first thing to understand when trying to identify why Guernsey is what it is.

The people of Guernsey are aware of their ancient French links but, by no means, do they identify themselves as anything other than British islanders.

Guernsey is a granite rock located in the Bay of St Malo. The nearest point of the French coast is just 20 miles away. On a clear day the cliffs and beaches of the Cotentin peninsula are clearly visible and, by night, the lights of the nuclear power station at Cap de Hague and the small towns in its shadow twinkle across the waters of the Alderney Race.

Guernsey is surrounded by deep waters and jagged rocks make themselves evident at low water. The Bay of St Malo has some of the biggest tidal flows in the world and the seascape of Guernsey looks dramatically different at either end of the tide.

For an island just six miles long by four miles wide Guernsey has a wide range of terrain and landscapes.

On the south coast of Guernsey there are dramatic cliffs looking out towards Jersey. The west coast has miles of beaches but there is nothing to see out there apart from seabirds and passing ships and the next landfall is the eastern seaboard of the United States.

In the north of the island there are extensive common lands with a large number of water-filled quarries as a legacy of a former major industry.

Guernsey is not just an island. It is an archipelago. It is part of a group of islands including Alderney, Sark, Brecqhou, Jethou, Herm and Lihou. There are also thousands of other rocks, most of which are invisible at high water. These dragon-toothed rocks make sailing the waters of the archipelago a challenge to seafarers.

There is no direct evidence that Guernsey was ever directly connected to the European mainland. Well, certainly not in the time that man has roamed the world. The first people who came to Guernsey had to come by boat. A situation that continued until the 1930s.

The first people who made the sea crossing were Neolithic men. There is evidence of Bronze Age settlements and later influences were introduced from Roman Gaul. Then came the Normans, then the British. For five years the Channel Islands came under German occupation.

The effects of all those settlements and visitations are easily visible all around the islands.

The people of Guernsey have made their living over the years by fishing, trading, privateering, quarrying, horticulture, tourism and, latterly, finance. Guernsey is a successful and widely-respected international finance centre.

The island of Guernsey has a population of

60,000, which makes for somewhat cosy living on an island just 25 miles square. However, there are still plenty of places where visitors and locals can seek out peace and quiet and where gulls can go to be lonely.

Guernsey is now a thriving place. Employment levels are exceptionally high, a property boom shows little sign of slackening and the population enjoys a very high standard of living. Taxation is a fixed 20% and there is no value added tax.

Dining out is a favourite island hobby and there are many splendid restaurants ready to satisfy the most discerning gourmet.

Although the general cost of living is high, eating out and enjoying good wine is relatively inexpensive compared to other areas of similar prosperity such as the south of England.

Guernsey enjoys an unusual relationship with the European Union. Neither member nor an associate the relationship is conducted entirely through the British government in Westminster. This has, to date, provided the canny people of Guernsey with a perfect solution to EU involvement – most of the benefits with few of the burdens.

In the meantime Guernsey and its sister islands offer beauty, style, gastronomy, history, fishing, flora and fauna, walking, sport and something of a lost British way of life flavoured with a subtle French residual influence.

On balance, a great place to live and to visit.

The **Guernsey flag** is a fairly recent invention. The flag features the red cross of St George with the cross of Normandy superimposed.

Meet the Ancestors

The first people to come to Guernsey came by boat. That is a proud boast for Guernseymen because their island was never connected to the continental landmass when there were people around.

They say that Guernseymen had to make an effort to get to their island whereas Jerseymen just stumbled onto theirs without getting their feet wet.

The first evidence of human habitation in Guernsey dates back to around 6,000 BC when hunting and fishing parties first landed on the island.

Excavations at Les Fouillages at L'Ancresse indicate that the first Guernsey settlements were established around 4,500 BC.

The islands eventually became part of the Roman Empire and the Romans did quite a lot for Guernsey. Well, perhaps not Romans but traders from Roman Gaul.

They started to come to the island around 100AD as Guernsey and Alderney became important staging points on journeys between Brittany and Britain.

The wreck of a Roman galley, now known as *Asterix*, was discovered in St Peter Port harbour in 1982.

As with so many things in Guernsey, the French connection is not quite as simple as the island's proximity to the Cotentin peninsula might suggest. The Cotentin is Norman and Guernsey's roots can be found there. It was the Normans, those descendants of the seagoing Norsemen the Vikings, who first established what could be described as authority over the island.

In 933 AD authority over the Channel Islands passed from Brittany to Normandy.

There is a widely-held belief in Guernsey that some of William the Conqueror's invasion fleet sailed from Guernsey on its way to Hastings. Guernseymen are rather proud of the part they played in the conquest of England in 1066.

King John, known as John Lackland, lived up to his nickname by losing most of England's remaining lands in France. In 1204 Guernsey opted to align with the English Crown rather than join France and that is the way things have stayed to this day.

In the following centuries Guernsey came under many religious influences but after the Reformation a strong Protestant ethic took root. Anglicanism, Presbyterianism, Calvinism and Methodism have all made an impact on the island. Guernsey even had the privilege of a visit from John Wesley preaching Methodism.

The puritan ethic led Guernsey to support Parliament against the King in the Civil War but loyalty to the Monarch, as Duke of Normandy, was soon re-established after the Restoration. That loyalty was not weakened during the German occupation and King George VI and Queen Elizabeth wasted no time in visiting Guernsey on 7 June 1945 just weeks after the liberation.

All these ancestral influences can be seen in the place and street names in Guernsey and the family names of the population. The French influences are very evident but the pronunciation of the names is, almost invariably, neither English nor French but distinctly Guernsey.

Guernsey has its own language, a version of Norman French. In typical, idiosyncratic, Guernsey manner this language differs from parish to parish.

The way things are said in Guernsey is not decided by government, church or committee but by the people themselves. That is the Guernsey way.

The Bailiwick

The islands of Guernsey are grouped together as a bailiwick. A bailiwick is a territory administered by a bailiff.

In the time of King John the government of the Channel Islands was under the control of a Lord of the Isles, the precursor to the title of bailiff.

The separation of Jersey and Guernsey into separate Bailiwicks can be traced back to 1204 when King John lost his possessions in continental Normandy but separate seals for the Bailiwicks were not eventually issued by Edward I until 1304.

At that time Alderney and Sark were established as part of the Bailiwick of Guernsey.

Alderney has its own parliament- the States of Deliberation.

Sark's legislature is known as Chief Pleas.

Guernsey's Bailiff remains as the chief citizen but the holder of the office's duties today are practically confined to serving as the head of the judiciary and presiding officer of the States of Deliberation, Guernsey's legislature.

That dual role has been questioned but can be distinguished from the disappearing office of Lord Chancellor in the United Kingdom as, unlike the Lord Chancellor, the Bailiff has no executive responsibility with political and executive power residing entirely in the elected members of the States.

Opposite
Pines on the southern cliffs.

Constitutional and external involvements

When the people of Guernsey get the chance to show their allegiance to the Crown they prove fiercely loyal.

Royal visits, Royal weddings and birthdays, bereavements and anniversaries are all marked with great gusto in the Bailiwick.

However, the relationship with the Monarchy is a strange one. Guernsey and the other Channel Islands have never been incorporated into the United Kingdom of Great Britain and Northern Island by conquest or by treaty. Instead, the islands represent the last Norman possessions of the Duke of Normandy. When William the Conqueror, the Duke of Normandy, became King of England he brought the Channel Islands with him and that remains the situation today.

It was in 1204 that King John finally lost the last of his Norman possessions in France and Guernsey and Jersey had to make a choice about

London being responsible for defence and international relations.

Sadly, the first time this was tested was in World War II when it was decided that the islands were indefensible against the German forces raging across Europe and they were abandoned to five long and difficult years of occupation.

The resumption of 'British' rule in 1945 led to the introduction of a new system of government.

In 1969 a Royal Commission was appointed to investigate and report on the constitutional relationship between the islands and the Crown. In October 1973 the Commission confirmed the convention that the Channel Islands are Crown dependencies with responsibility for their own internal affairs but with the United Kingdom retaining responsibility for external relations.

This report, the Kilbrandon Report, also confirmed

Guernsey's Royal Court House. This elegant setting serves as court room and parliamentary chamber. The Royal Court convenes here and once a month it is given over to meetings of the States of Deliberation.

which way to go. They opted to follow their Duke of Normandy and place their allegiance with him rather than throw in their lot with France.

Over the centuries the relationship with France has been a difficult one with invasions, incursions and incidents but the gradual Anglicisation of the islands and the triumph of the English language have firmly cemented Guernsey and the other islands with the British sovereign.

The convention developed that the islands acted independently but with the UK government in

that the islands held their link with the Crown through the Dukes of Normandy. The people of the Channel Islands are not subject to the British government but owe their allegiance to the Crown.

However, not all UK politicians and civil servants were happy to allow the islands such a free rein. The idea stalked the corridors of Whitehall that the islands should not take an independent line on any issues that made them look very different from the UK.

It soon became apparent that in the event of any

conflicts that could not be resolved the UK government would have the right of decision. This was not universally accepted in Guernsey as it was felt that Guernsey's relationship was with the Crown and not the government.

A dramatic change in that relationship came about when Great Britain signed the Treaty of Accession to the Treaty of Rome and became a member of the European Economic Community. The special trading status of the islands and the relationship with the UK would be seriously affected when the UK entered the EEC. The British government offered the islanders the option of full independence but another route was sought.

Special terms were negotiated for the Channel Islands which proved to be just as advantageous

ratified by the Westminster parliament and then sent to Guernsey to be confirmed by the States of Deliberation. This led to ludicrous events such as a treaty to allow relief columns on their way to Bosnia being allowed free access to ports and roads being ratified in Guernsey and then being sent on to Sark for ratification by Chief Pleas. This caused some amusement in Sark where the only transport is by foot, tractor, horse or bicycle.

As well as concerns about Europe a new attitude to the islands by the Labour government elected in 1997 became evident. Great offence was caused in the islands when the British government announced a review of the financial regulatory system in the islands without any prior consultation.

Following on from this Edwards Report, attention

The **Royal Coat of Arms.**

as it was possible to imagine. Under the terms of Protocol 3 to the Treaty of Accession the Channel Islands were allowed access to European markets on a free-trade basis and most Channel Islanders were granted the right to work in the EEC.

This seemed a win-win situation for the islands and whilst the EEC continued to be perceived as an economic entity this worked most successfully.

However, as the EEC became the European Union and the implications of ever-closer political union became apparent alarm bells started to ring.

EU legislation eventually became pre-eminent of British law and decisions of the EU had to be

has been focused on the financial services in the islands by the Organisation for Economic Co-operation and Development and the International Monetary Fund.

The British Government also announced the creation of an Anglo-Irish Council as part of its Northern Ireland peace initiative. Guernsey and Jersey are involved in this and, again, this was done without any prior consultation.

The stated intention to place Britain at the heart of Europe is causing concern in the Channel Islands. The offer of independence apparently made by the British government in the 1970s might come up for discussion again in the near future.

Government House is the residence of the Lieutenant-Governor of Guernsey, the Queen's official representative.

The States of Deliberation

Guernsey has its own parliament called the States of Deliberation.

The history of the States, as they are locally and colloquially known, dates back to the early 17th century but the modern manifestation has resulted from the need to produce a new form of island government at the end of the German occupation in 1945.

During the occupation the Bailiff and the States were nominally still the government but the administration was in the hands of a body called the Controlling Committee. A new-look government had to be introduced after the war. The States of Deliberation after the war was comprised of elected Deputies, 12 Conseillers and 10 representatives from the Parish douzaines. The Conseillers were experienced and senior politicians elected by the deputies.

One of the problems Guernsey's system of democracy has had in recent years has been in getting people to vote. It is necessary to apply to get onto the electoral roll and many people just do not bother.

In 1994 it was decided to reform the system by having the Conseillers directly elected by the people on an islandwide basis. This did stimulate a good electoral turnout at the first election. It also resulted in the election to the 'top bench' of several populist politicians who did not conform to the old 'great and the good' profile of Conseillers.

This was too much for Guernsey's 'Old Guard' politicians who, in 2000, were able with the support of the douzaine representatives to have the post of Conseiller abolished.

By 2001 a sense that it was time to reform the States became widely apparent, particularly in the business sector.

A plan for a new style of government, with the end of the committee system and presidents and the introduction of departments and ministers, was approved in 2003 for introduction the next year.

Sadly, by the middle of 2003, because of a perceived lack of action or unwillingness to make decisions, the standing of the States in the public estimation was probably at an all-time low.

At a time when the future of the island seemed under the greatest threat since 1940, the decisive leadership required was widely felt to be absent.

Civil War

Although the English Civil War was mostly about the King and Parliament, Channel Islanders found their own reasons for dispute. Local rivalries and family ambitions resulted in Guernsey and Jersey taking opposing sides in the war between Roundheads and Cavaliers.

Jersey sided with the King and Guernsey, with its Calvanist, more puritan religious element declared for Parliament.

Some might say that the distinction is still apparent today with Jersey's slightly raffish air contrasting with the more staid way of life in Guernsey. Certainly, it was not until the 21st century that Guernsey showed signs of being open for any kind of business on Sunday.

Even that simple alignment between the two warring factions was too uncomplicated a concept for Guernsey to accept. Just to make life particularly interesting Castle Cornet, commanding the entrance to St Peter Port, remained in the hands of the Royalists and was supplied by boat from Jersey.

The castle was besieged for eight years and nine months and only surrendered in December 1651 after Jersey had fallen to Parliament's forces.

During the long years of the war the besieged garrison in the castle regularly fired its cannons into St Peter Port just a few hundred yards away. Some of the more entrepreneurial citizens of the town used to collect the cannon balls and sell them back to the castle's gunners.

There was a Guernsey contingent prominent in the Parliamentary forces that ended Jersey's involvement in the Civil War. Unfortunately, that contingent gained a considerable reputation for looting. Yet another reason for the strong feelings between the islands that usually manifest themselves during the annual inter-island Muratti Vase football match.

The view from the ramparts of **Castle Cornet** still commands the town.

Occupation and Liberation

One of the first arrivals at Guernsey's new airport at La Villaize was not very welcome.

On 30 June 1940 a lone German pilot landed at the new airport, had a look around, realised that the island was not going to resist invasion and then took off to report back to his superiors. Later that day a group of Junker transporters landed a platoon of Luftwaffe troops.

These events ushered in five long years of German occupation of the Bailiwick of Guernsey. The decision had been made, as the German panzers swept across France, that the islands could not be defended and had to be demilitarised. All British troops left and there was a partial evacuation by those civilians who felt they could not stay.

Many children were sent away. Ironically, some of them went to places such as Southampton, Plymouth and Glasgow where they proved to be in greater danger from bombing than they would have been if they had stayed in Guernsey.

The grim corridors of the **German underground hospital**. This is a much-visited tourist site.

The German garrison soon made its presence felt. The German language was to be taught in schools, Occupation Reischmarks would replace sterling as currency and all traffic would have to travel on the right-hand side of the road.

Although Adolf Hitler never came to Guernsey he was obsessed with his success at conquering a piece of British territory. He had great belief in his own military genius and saw the islands as unsinkable aircraft carriers or battleships from which he could deter or destroy the British fleet. He ordered the building of huge fortifications and gun emplacements which never fired a shot in anger. These constructions did play a significant part in the liberation of Europe. Every gun deployed and every ton of concrete poured was an asset diverted from the Atlantic Wall. It could be said that the excessive German expenditure on the defences of the islands played an important part in the D-Day landings just because they were in the wrong place.

Although the government of the island remained nominally in the hands of the Bailiff and the States of Deliberation during the occupation, the real authority as liaison with the occupying power was vested in the Controlling Committee.

The Committee did its best to work with the Germans to make life as tolerable as possible for the islands but the next five years were tough. There were restrictions placed on the islanders' ability to go fishing. Listening to the radio was banned and the local newspaper become subject to censorship.

Despite all this the occupation was fairly benign. For the German soldiers, being part of the occupying force in the Channel Islands was far preferable to the prospect of a short and brutish life on the Eastern Front.

After the D-Day landings and the liberation of the nearby coasts of France, things took a turn for the worst.

Shortly after 6 June 1944 the Germans lost the ability to adequately support their forces in the island by sea. There is a story that Winston Churchill was asked what should be done about the cut-off Germans in the islands. His reply was typically firm and abrupt.

"*Let them starve,*" he growled. Unfortunately, the islanders then had to share in the privations. There are still some elderly Guernsey residents who cannot forget or forgive that they could look out at the liberated shores of France for eleven long months while they faced starvation.

During these grim times occupiers and occupied became desperate for food. Every root vegetable on the island suddenly become a delicacy and the islanders found their cats and dogs going

missing as the German soldiers desperately searched for some meat to enhance their limited diet.

Late in 1944 agreement was reached through the Red Cross to allow the Red Cross ship *SS Vega* to bring supplies to the starving islanders.

Eventually the day of liberation drew near. On 8 May 1945 Churchill broadcast to the nation to announce that the war in Europe was coming to an end. Guernsey people recovered the hidden radios from the shed or under the baby's pram and listened enthralled as Churchill declared that the ceasefire had been sounded all along the fronts "and our dear Channel Islands will be freed today."

On 9 May Task Force *HMS Bulldog* arrived in St Peter Port Harbour to take the surrender of the German garrison and Brigadier Snow stood on the steps outside the Royal Court House to proclaim that the occupation was at an end. A bank holiday was declared to mark the first Liberation Day, and 9 May is still officially celebrated as such to this day.

The islanders wasted no time in removing as many signs of occupation as possible. German gun emplacements and bunkers were destroyed and guns and equipment tipped into the sea.

There was so much German material in the islands that there was plenty to retain, and under the auspices of the Fortress Guernsey project many emplacements and pieces of wartime memorabilia have been restored to provide examples of living history for islanders and visitors.

Although the liberation was a long time ago and most of those involved have faded away, Liberation Day has assumed a new status as Guernsey's national day. Anyone in the Bailiwick on 9 May will soon realise the importance of the memories it invokes for the survivors of World War II and its significance to a newer generation.

Pleinmont from the sea. There would have been little chance of making an opposed landing up these cliffs.

When the tomato was king

Approaching Guernsey from the air it is impossible to miss the sight of thousands of greenhouses glimmering like water in the sun. These are the legacy of one of the foundations of Guernsey's prosperity – the tomato industry. Tomatoes were first grown in Guernsey in the 1860s as an adjunct to growing grapes, a major export at the time, and by the 1890s the tomato industry was well on its way to becoming the mainstay of the island's economy. By 1939 over 35,000 tons of tomatoes were being exported annually.

After the war the industry soon dusted itself down and was restored to full heath within two years. In 1947 more than 7 million of the distinctive chip baskets, each containing 12 pounds of tomatoes, were exported. The baskets lived on in island life long after their original purpose was completed, pressed into service for uses as diverse as tool boxes or taking tea onto the beach in the afternoon.

In the 1960s there were very few Guernseymen who did not have a few feet of glass where they grew their tomatoes. The decline of the industry set in when competition from the Netherlands and Spain undercut the Guernsey product in UK shops and supermarkets. The Dutch tomatoes were grown in heated greenhouses but, unlike the Guernsey growers, their fuel was subsidised by their government. The 'hobby' growers were the first to go out of business but many of the commercial growers soon followed.

The history of the Guernsey tomato can be glimpsed all around the island by the sad sight of overgrown and neglected greenhouses waiting for the next winter gale to knock them down, or – the greenhouse owner's dream – permission to redevelop the site for housing or commercial building.

The signs of decay and dereliction are everywhere but, in the spirit of perversity that controls politics in Guernsey, one of the largest and most modern greenhouse complexes was sold in 2003 to be re-developed as two schools. Other industries have left their mark on the island. Farming has played a large part in Guernsey's economic life. The Guernsey cow is world famous for the quality of its milk and the breed has been successfully established around the world. Guernsey herds can be found in South Africa, New Zealand, Canada and the United States.

An island that is made of granite was obviously going to attract the attention of the quarrying industry. The northern part of the island is rich in blue granite which was perfect for road building and for the facings of buildings, but today the industry has dwindled away to almost nothing. The marks of it are clear to see with many old quarries now filled with water, some of which are used for the island's water supply. Others have been employed to take the ever-increasing piles of refuse.

Guernsey people have always been seafarers and the island has supported a substantial fishing fleet in the past. In the 17th century Guernsey fishermen were working the cod banks of Newfoundland at the mouth of the St Lawrence River. Over the years styles and target species have changed and in recent times the Guernsey fishing fleet has concentrated on shellfish such as lobsters and spider crabs, mostly for sale in the French and Spanish markets.

Unfortunately, other fishing fleets have been looking for different fish using different methods. Trawlers and potters cannot co-exist and there have been many cases of Guernsey fishermen losing their pots as giant stern trawlers have rampaged through the fishing grounds.

Disputes about fishing rights have been a source of rancour with the French neighbours for many years. French boats have been arrested in disputed waters around the Bailiwick and brought into St Peter Port. On many occasions the skippers have been tried, fined and had their catch confiscated.

The Guernsey Fisheries Committee obtained a specialised fisheries protection vessel, *Leopardess*, to police Guernsey's fishing territory. This has been involved in several confrontations with French fishing boats. The French have not taken kindly to this. They have disputed the rights claimed by Guernsey fishermen and even the legitimacy of the Guernsey Court under European law.

In one famous case in 1993, 39 French vessels 'invaded' St Peter Port harbour to protest against the arrest of a French trawler. This was a considerable show of strength and concentrated many minds on how these long-running disputes must be handled in the future. In all the negotiations about the future of the EU's Common Fisheries Policy the interests of Guernsey's fishing fleet are not likely to get much of a hearing. The only thing that can be said with any certainty is that disputes between French and Guernsey fishermen will continue much as they have for centuries.

Guernsey issues its own version of sterling currency but the islanders remain very attached to the pound note and are extremely reluctant to use pound coins.

The Finance Industry

Guernsey's status as an international finance centre has been responsible for the island's present day wealth.

Jersey led the way in the early 1970s by utilising its status as a low tax-area to attract banking business. It was said that in those days Aurigny pilots flying into Guernsey from Jersey told their passengers to put their watches back 10 years on landing. That may have been accurate for a while but Guernsey soon caught up.

Banking, tax planning, investment business and trust management were all attracted to the islands by the tax advantages available. Most of the main United Kingdom high street banks had branches in the islands but they soon expanded their operations into an international context.

International banks were not slow to appreciate how significant the Channel Islands could be as bases for international private banking. Major international operators such as The Royal Bank of Canada and Credit Suisse chose to use Guernsey as their bases in the Channel Islands and many international banks decided to operate in both bailiwicks.

By the end of 2002 there were 67 banks licensed in Guernsey with £71.9 billion on deposit.

Guernsey is a world leader in captive insurance management and is the leading centre in Europe for this type of business.

There is a thriving investment management business in Guernsey with more than £33 billion under management in 2002.

The engine of most of this business has been fiduciary services. Trust and company management has become an island speciality.

The licensing of fiduciaries was one of the

recommendations of the Edwards Report but Guernsey was already making plans to do this and a system was put in place during 2002 and 2003. Guernsey is one of the first offshore jurisdictions to have such a regime operating. Guernsey prides itself on being a well-regulated financial jurisdiction with the responsibility for policing its activities undertaken by the Guernsey Financial Services Commission. The Bailiwick's system of financial regulation has been praised by the International Monetary Fund and the Organisation for Economic Co-operation and Development.

Finance is now the Bailiwick's major income producer with some 7,000 of the population employed in the sector.

The **Admiral Park** development at **Les Banques** is now home to two major banking operations.

Helvetia Court was constructed as offices for Credit Suisse, one of the largest employers in Guernsey.

The Ruling Class

There is a saying in Guernsey that the Careys speak to the Brocks, the Brocks speak to the De Saumarez but the De Saumarez only speak to God.

These and several other prominent families have played important roles in Guernsey's history. The Guernsey story is liberally sprinkled with contributions from the Brock, Carey, de Saumarez, Ozanne, le Patourel and le Pelley families.

Admiral Lord de Saumarez was one of the most distinguished naval commanders of his time. As a junior officer he served on board HMS *Victory*. In 1794 he commanded a squadron escorting cargo vessels to England when his flotilla encountered five French frigates just north-west of Guernsey. His ships fought a delaying action which enabled the vulnerable packets to escape and then he used his and his crew's local knowledge to sail his ship, HMS *Crescent*, perilously close to the rocks and reefs around the north of Guernsey. The French could not lay a gun on him as they tried to follow whilst avoiding the rocks and the shore batteries. He completed an extraordinary manoeuvre to pass through channels that many thought impassable and he brought his ship safely into St Peter Port harbour. Lord de Saumarez served as Lord Nelson's second-in-command at the Battle of the Nile and received a wealth of awards for gallantry before being raised to the peerage.

Daniel de Lisle Brock served as Bailiff of Guernsey from 1821-1842. He gained a reputation as a fierce champion of the rights of Guernsey and Guernseymen in the face of the overweening power of the government in London.

His brother, Sir Isaac Brock, earned his reputation in an entirely different field. Isaac Brock is known as the Hero of Upper Canada.

Sir Isaac fought in the war with America of 1812, leading a force that captured Detroit. He then defeated an American invading force at Queenstown Heights near Niagara Falls. Brock was killed in the battle but Canada was saved for the King.

A giant monumental column to his achievements now stands on the bluff at Queenstown Heights looking down towards Niagara on the lake and Toronto in the distance. Brock University in Ontario was named in his honour and a bursary is offered there to enable a Guernsey student to study in Canada.

Victor Carey had the unenviable task of being Bailiff and Lieutenant-Governor during the German occupation of Guernsey. His grandson, Sir de Vic Carey, followed in his footsteps as Bailiff in 1999.

The name de Carteret is most prominent in the history of Sark. Helier de Carteret originally obtained the fiefdom of Sark from Queen Elizabeth I. The de Carteret family dominated the island with several men called Philippe de Carteret acting as Bailiff. The family hold on Sark was fatally broken when Sir Philippe de Carteret backed the losing side in the English Civil War. There was another de Carteret prominent in recent Sark history. Laurence de Carteret, who runs Sark's power station, was Seneschal of the island for 18 years.

Next time you are at Gatwick Airport and taking refreshment remember another famous Guernseyman. William le Lacheur was the man who founded the Costa Rican coffee trade.

Guernseymen and their families have made a significant contribution to British history as well as moulding and shaping the life of their home island.

The **Commodore Clipper** arrives from Portsmouth, en route to Jersey.

Trains, Boats and Planes

The most essential ingredient for the survival of a thriving island community is its connections with the outside world.

Over the generations Guernsey has forged links to the United Kingdom and France by sea and airline with the railways, bizarrely, contributing a significant chapter to the transport history.

During the great age of steam, railway companies also ran shipping services. In the 1840s the London and South Western Railway started to operate steamers from Poole to the Channel Islands and France. The grounding of a ferry in Poole Harbour ended that service and ensured that Poole remained out of favour as a port to serve the Channel Islands for another 120 years. In August 1850 the LSWR started a service from Weymouth to Guernsey, Jersey, Granville and St Malo. It was not a success and the LSWR switched its attentions to Southampton.

Once adequate rail connections were made to Weymouth it became the main port for the Channel Islands, a status maintained for many years.

The regular daily mail boats were a feature of Channel Islands life for more than a century. The arrival and departure of each ship was an important event with lists of those leaving the island or visiting being published in the local newspapers. This practice is said to have ended after a certain Guernsey dignitary was reported as having left for Weymouth in company with a woman with whom he should not have been travelling.

Ferry services were much reduced during the First World War and were an early casualty of World War II with a string of vessels evacuating thousands of islanders shortly before the Germans landed to commence the Occupation in June 1940.

After the war and liberation a limited cargo service got underway in September 1945 but it was not until June 1946 that passenger service was restored.

The post-war Labour government had ambitions to control the commanding heights of the economy and the railways were identified as prime targets. In December 1947 all the railway companies were nationalised and their ferry services became part of the new British Railways. Probably the two most famous vessels of the BR era were *Caesarea* and *Sarnia*. These were the last conventional ferries built for the Channel Islands service and each was designed to carry 1,400 passengers. *Caesarea* and *Sarnia* continued in service until 1976 and 1978 respectively. By then the BR fleet had been re-branded as Sealink.

Cargo traffic had declined dramatically by then as Guernsey's tomato exporting industry went into decline.

The need to be able to transport cars ushered in the age of the roll-on, roll-off ferry. *Earl Godwin* and *Earl William* continued to serve the islands until Sealink was sold to Sea Containers Limited. There was a short period of competition with a service provide by British Channel Island Ferries but, eventually, all the old ships were phased out of the islands. Today Guernsey is served by Condor Ferries high-speed catamarans, combined with their passenger and freight vessels.

Guernsey's first airport was operated from L'Eree on the south-west coast from 1931. The current airport was completed and opened in 1940 just in time for the arrival of the Luftwaffe.

Guernsey has also had a chequered history with air services. Over the years many operators have come and gone and it is widely said in aviation circles that nobody has ever made any money on the Channel Islands routes.

British European Airways, Eagle Airways, Channel Islands Air Services, Air UK, KLMuk and British Airways are all names that were once familiar at Guernsey Airport but are now gone. The vast majority of Guernsey's air passengers are now carried by Flybe, an airline owned by the family trusts of the late Jack Walker.

Guernsey suffered a severe blow in 1998 when KLMuk withdrew its service between Guernsey and London Heathrow, selling off its landing slots in the process. Guernsey had lost its link to London's major airport.

In 2003 BA pulled out of Gatwick and offered to hand over the service to local airline Aurigny. Aurigny has operated in the Channel Islands for more than 30 years, providing a lifeline inter-island service using, mostly, Britten-Norman Islanders and Trislanders.

Guernsey's government then stepped in, bought Aurigny and now Guernsey has a nationalised airline and, hopefully, has secured the Gatwick route permanently.

Guernsey's own airline, **Aurigny**, competes for business with its rival **Flybe**.

St Peter Port

St Peter Port is truly the jewel in the crown of Guernsey. In fact, it has a strong claim to be the most picturesque place in the whole of the Channel Islands.

The approach to the town from the sea is spectacular, the streets and buildings rising up from the seafront along the hill.

St Peter Port has always been the gateway to Guernsey and the town started to come into being early in the 13th century – the same century in which work commenced on the building of the imposing Castle Cornet. The castle dominates the approach into the harbour and was originally an island – a fact which resulted in the extraordinary state of affairs whereby the castle remained in Royalist hands throughout the English Civil War whilst Guernsey itself, just a few hundred yards away, was in Parliamentary hands. The castle was eventually connected to the shore by a causeway completed in 1859.

The earliest signs of building in St Peter Port were Roman remains found in La Plaiderie in 1984.

St Peter Port is unusual for a town of its age, as it never had a town wall as such – the extent of the town was marked by stones called barrières. It developed as a major trading port and this trade reached its apogee in the 18th century. Guernsey merchants got rich during this time and they had substantial houses built. These can be seen in areas of the town such as Queen's Road, Les Gravees and The Grange.

Some of these fine properties are no longer private homes. A splendid town house in Le Pollet is now Moore's Central Hotel. The former home of Sir Isaac Brock, the hero of Upper Canada, is a branch of Boots and Warwick House in the Grange is home to the Guernsey Sporting Club. From 1855-1870, during his exile from his homeland, one famous home in Hauteville was the residence of the great French writer Victor Hugo. During his time in Guernsey he wrote two of his most famous novels, *Les Miserables* and *Les Travailleurs de la Mer*, the latter set in Guernsey. Hauteville House, given to the City of Paris, is now operated as a museum.

The merchant trade was possible because of the development of St Peter Port's fine harbour in stages over the centuries. The original harbour walls have now been built on and the seafront is much farther away from the heart of the town. Traces of the old harbour can be glimpsed through the walkways leading up from the seafront into the High Street.

A major redevelopment of the seafront in the 1980s involved a massive reclamation scheme at the North Beach to create a new marina and car parking.

For many years, a central aspect of Guernsey life was the town markets. There were flourishing fruit and vegetable stalls, butchers' shops and, of course, fishmongers. This was where islanders came in their hundreds; not just to shop, but to meet each other, keep in touch and exchange news and views of island life.

The early St Peter Port market was held in the streets around the town church. The decision was made to house the market in purpose-built buildings and work started on these in 1777. The completion of the project was financed by the issue of States' notes at no interest.

The markets thrived for many years but in the 1980s and 1990s decline set in and the market buildings have now been let on a long lease to a commercial developer with the intention of restoring them and bringing business back to this area.

St Peter Port also has a thriving shopping area in the Commercial Arcades. These were constructed by a Jersey-born developer, who became bankrupt in the process, in the 1830s. Not surprisingly, his plans for a glass roof over the Arcades never came to fruition.

Many new developments have been undertaken in St Peter Port in recent years to house the burgeoning finance sector. Some of these, such as Helvetia House and Elizabeth House, have been welcomed as examples of sensitive development enhancing the appearance of the town, but other recent developments have not proved so popular with islanders.

Summer bustle in the High Street with St Peter's Church, known as the Town Church in the distance.

Marinas and moorings are big business in Guernsey for locals and visitors.

Spirit of Guernsey – the island's lifeboat. The local branch of the RNLI took delivery of this Severn class vessel in 1997 after £1m was raised locally for its purchase.

Castle Cornet illuminates the night sky of Guernsey. It was illuminated in a different way in December 1672 when lightning struck the magazine, killing the Governor's wife and his mother-in-law. The Governor was elsewhere at the time.

Opposite page
The battery at **Castle Cornet**. From here loyal salutes are fired on the Sovereign's official birthday and Liberation Day.

Behind the ramparts at Castle Cornet.

From fort to castle: The view of **Castle Cornet** from **Fort George**. The Castle houses a fine museum and gallery and stages open-air theatre productions in the summer.

The **noonday gun** is fired from the ramparts daily throughout the summer months.

Opposite page
The **Condor** fast ferries are the principal method of sea travel for people and cars between Guernsey, Jersey, England and France.

Cruise liners such as **Oriana** (pictured here) and **Aurora** are regular visitors to St Peter Port. Many passengers come ashore to tour the island and visit the shops and restaurants.

The **Condor Ferries** vessels *Commodore Goodwill* and *Commodore Clipper* (pictured here) carry most of the produce in and out of the island. When the winter winds blow too hard for the fast ferries to take to sea, they also carry the people and cars that would otherwise be stranded.

St James Concert Hall is the centre of Guernsey's artistic life. Here, internationally renowned names such as Vladimir Ashkenazy, Willard White, Evelyn Glennie, Julian Lloyd Webber and Jacques Lousier have performed in recent times. St James was once a church and was marked for redevelopment. In a remarkable display of people power, a local group of dedicated art lovers campaigned to get the redevelopment idea overturned and to have the church converted into a cultural centre.

Guernsey also has a very high standard of local musicians and singers, and concerts featuring local choirs and orchestras, often working with very distinguished guest performers, are usually sell-outs.

St James also houses Guernsey's Millennium Tapestry, designed and produced by all the island's parishes.

Elizabeth College is Guernsey's pre-eminent boys' school accepting a mix of scholarship and paid pupils. The school was founded in 1563 on the instructions of Queen Elizabeth I. Old Elizabethans have played, and continue to play, important roles in all aspects of Guernsey life.

Victoria Tower was built in 1848 to commemorate Queen Victoria's surprise visit to Guernsey in 1846. If you want to see the wonderful view from the top the nearby fire brigade has the keys.

The statue of **Victor Hugo** in Candie Gardens. The great French writer and polemicist lived in Guernsey from 1855 to 1870 during his exile from his homeland. In Guernsey he wrote *Les Miserables* and *Les Travailleurs de la Mer.*

Candie Gardens. A floral touch in St Peter Port.

Smith Street, St Peter Port dressed for summer. Many of Guernsey's streets, roads and places have split personalities. Two names for a location are quite common. Smith Street is also La Rue des Forges.

The statue of **Prince Albert** commemorates his surprise visit to Guernsey with Queen Victoria in 1846.

It pays to look up in **St Peter Port**. There is some remarkable architecture above eye level.

Pedestrians only in this part of Town.

The **Town Markets** were once the heart of commerce and communication in Guernsey.

A truly family business. Five generations of the Randall family have been brewing beer at **Vauxlaurens** since 1873.

Sir Thomas de la Rue was one of Guernsey's most significant entrepreneurs. The company he founded is world famous for printing bank notes, newspapers and producing playing cards. His memory is marked on the wall of a popular public house in St Peter Port.

Opposite page
St Peter Port is a steep town with several sets of steps connecting the various levels. **Constitution Steps** lead to Sunnycroft Hotel and then on up to Clifton, but it is a hard climb.

A familiar sight in summer is a luxury cruise liner standing off from **Castle Cornet**.

Thatch on a cliff top is somewhat unusual but there are several fine examples in Guernsey. This view takes in the Governor's steps previously used for access to the bay.

The garrison cemetery at **Fort George**. Here lie the bodies of British soldiers and their families from the time of the garrisoning of the island by the British army. This cemetery also contains the graves of German soldiers who died in Guernsey during the Occupation.

The Bluebell Woods are a favourite place for walks in the spring.

Fermain Bay on Guernsey's south coast. This beautiful bay used to be accessible from St Peter Port by ferry. Now you have to walk there but it is worth it.

The **Pepper Pot** above Fermain Bay is a useful mark for mariners.

Opposite page
Perhaps not quite a pine 'forest' but that is how it is known in Guernsey.

La Gran'Mere du Chimquierie guards the gate to **St Martin's Church**. This venerable old lady probably dates back to around 3,000 B.C. and may be a relic of an Earth Mother culture.

Following pages
Daffodils on the cliffs with **Herm** and **Jethou** in the background.

Hedge-veg is an old Guernsey tradition. It evolved from growers disposing of excess stock from unmanned stalls at the roadside. It relies entirely on trust that the customer will put the right money in the tin or box alongside the stall.

The parish boundaries between **St Peter Port** and **St Martin's** are marked near Damouettes Lane by an abreveur, a horse trough.

St Martin's Point below Idlerocks Hotel. A favourite fishing place for locals and visitors.

The spectacular beach at **Petit Port**. Very private and difficult to access.

Petit Port is best visited by boat these days. The very steep steps are no longer maintained as they used to be.

SPIRIT OF GUERNSEY

The **Little Chapel** at **Les Vauxbelets** is one of Guernsey's most popular tourist attractions. The construction of the chapel was started by Brother Deodat, a monk of the De La Salle Christian Brothers order, as a miniature replica of Notre Dame de Lourdes.

Torteval is farming country, both indoors and out.

The **Guernsey cow** is famous around the world for the richness of its milk.

Exporting flowers is now an important part of Guernsey farming.

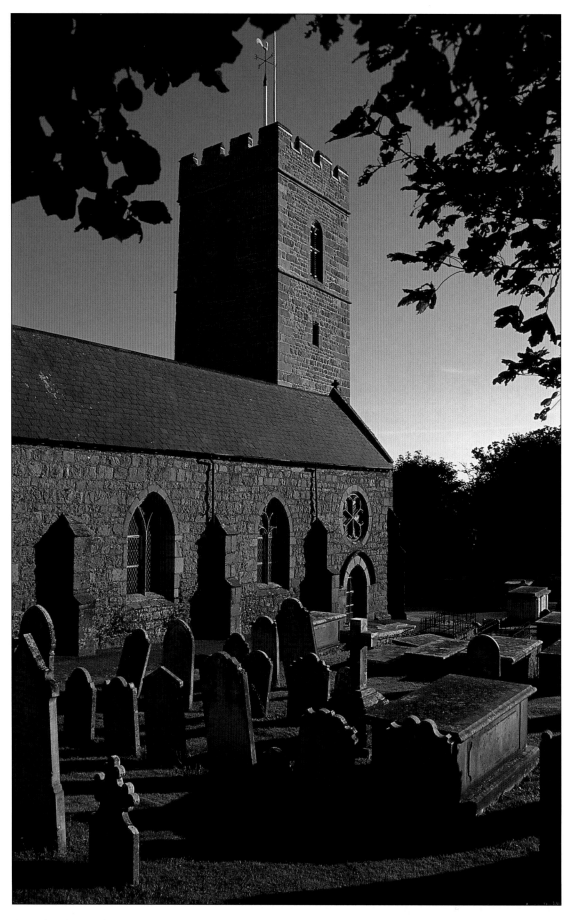

The parish church of **St Pierre du Bois**.

Torteval Church. The most soulful skies are always out west.

Hitler's Atlantic Wall was extended into Guernsey and Alderney but never fired a shot in anger.

Mont Herault Watch-house. A neighbouring watch-house, long demolished, featured as a haunted house in Victor Hugo's *Travailleurs de la Mer*.

The watch on the cliffs.

Hanois light. Once a home to a lighthouse keeper but now fully automated.

Fort Grey is known as the Cup and Saucer and houses a maritime museum focussing on shipwrecks.

Following pages
L'Erée headland looks out towards Lihou island.

Le Trepied dolmen at **La Catioroc, St Saviour's**. The word dolmen comes from the Breton '*table of stone.*' This was also a meeting place for witches.

Previous pages
Vazon Bay on the west coast with Fort Hommet in the distance.

St Apolline's Chapel was built in 1392. It is believed to be the only church or chapel dedicated to St Apolline, the patron saint of dentists. The chapel contains an important fresco depicting the Last Supper. The chapel has had a chequered history, falling into sad states of decay at times. It was once used as a cattle stable.

St Saviour's reservoir is the catchment area for much of Guernsey's rainwater and a quiet place for walking, birdwatching and trout fishing.

Guernsey's millennium project was the construction of a walk around the St Saviour's reservoir.

The main lake at St Pierre Park Hotel is a good place to see herons and kingfishers.

St Pierre Park Hotel was built on 44 acres of land in the 1970s on the site of the Vimiera college for novices.

The nine-hole golf course at St Pierre Park Hotel was designed by double Open champion Tony Jacklin.

You can easily tell the name of this property at **King's Mills**. If you want a self-catering holiday with your wisteria this is the place for you.

The **de Saumarez bridge** was built to connect the family estate across a main road so the children could get to school safely.

Opposite page
St John Residential Home at Saumarez Park.

Sand racing is one of the noisier activities on the beach at **Chouet**.

Horse riding is a quieter alternative.

The beach and the rocks at **Cobo**.

The broad sweep of Guernsey's **west coast**.

Fort Hommet is a Martello tower that was altered and adapted by the German occupation force for their own purposes as strongpoint Rotenstein. It contains a renovated gun casement.

Where jackboots once marched.

Top
The sun may be sinking into the sea but a new one will be coming up over Sark in the morning.

 87

Reflections on a silvery sea.

The distinctive pink granite of Guernsey's west coast at **Saline Bay**.

The seawall at **Vazon**. Spring tides and high winds can make the coast road impassable along here.

A good vantage point at **Le Guet**.

The church of **St Michel du Valle**. The Vale church looms large over the north of the island and the bay at Grand Havre.

Sea pinks in profusion.

Once a coastal defence but now a roost for pigeons.

L'Ancresse Common is home to the **Royal Guernsey Golf Club** and **L'Ancresse Golf Club**. This par 70 links course is a serious test of golf. With sea on three sides there is always a wind blowing, the fairways are narrow, the gorse is waiting and some of the bunkers were built by Germans, but not with golf in mind. The course record is 64.

High and dry.

Baie de la Jaonneuse.

The northern beaches are perfect for paddling and pottering around pools.

Guernsey's shooting ranges are located here near the isolated **Fort Marchant**.

Not a Martello tower but constructed for the same purpose. These coastal defences were built during the American War of Independence when the French had sided with the revolutionaries.

Looking over **L'Ancresse** and the **Vale**.

The stark **Fort Doyle** at the north of the island is a significant place for birdwatchers on the lookout for migrants and vagrants.

Following pages
Inside the **Dehus dolmen** at **Bordeaux**. This probably dates back to around 3,300 BC and is alleged to be haunted by a nocturnal spectre.

Beaucette Marina was once a quarry. A hole was blasted in a wall to let in the sea and create this haven for yachts and houseboats.

Petils Bay looking out towards Herm and Jethou over the light at La Platte.

Opposite page
Bordeaux Harbour is a favourite mooring for local boaters and fishermen.

Until 1806 Guernsey was two islands. The northern part of the island was separated from the main part by a strip of water called **La Braye du Valle**. As part of the military preparations organised by Sir John Doyle the area was drained and the **Clos du Valle** connected to **St Sampson's**. This area at St Sampson's is still known as The Bridge.

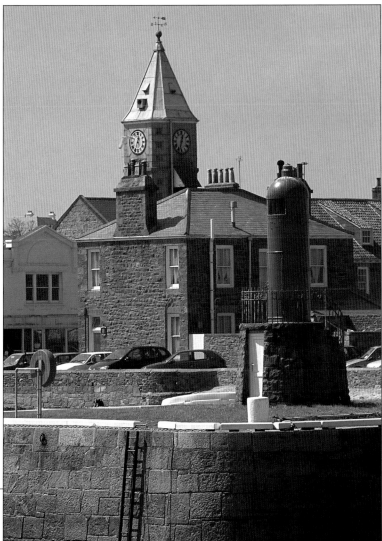

The harbour at **St Sampson's**.

Herm, the Islanders' Island

Just across the water from St Peter Port is the island of Herm. This can fairly be called the Guernseyman's playground. On any sunny morning or peaceful evening the waters of the Little Russell are speckled with boats as a friendly invasion sets out from Guernsey to the small island three miles across the water.

Herm is an island just a mile and a half long and half a mile wide. It is owned by Guernsey but has been let out on a long lease to the Wood family since 1949.

Under the far-sighted guidance of the late Major Wood and his wife Jenny the island has been transformed from a ramshackle near-ruin to a delightful holiday destination catering for day visitors, discerning diners and a loyal band of regular returnees enjoying weekend breaks or summer holidays.

Herm has had a colourful history and some colourful residents, including the Carthusian Order, Prince Blucher von Wahlstatt, Sir Compton Mackenzie and a colony of wallabies.

In the past the island has had a thriving farm, an oyster farming business and there was even an attempt to establish a golf course. That latter enterprise proved to be a battle between golfers and rabbits in which the rabbits emerged triumphant.

At the end of the Second World War Herm was in a sorry state. It had been largely abandoned during the war with just a caretaker there and occasional periods of occupation by German troops.

Major Wood and his wife came to the island, fell in love with what they saw, recognised the potential and made arrangements to acquire the property.

In times past Herm had been Crown Property and been used by Governors of Guernsey as their private hunting territory., and in 1946 Guernsey bought Herm from the Crown with the aim of establishing it as a tourism amenity.

The Woods came to an agreement with the then tenant Alfred Graham Jefferies and they convinced the Guernsey authorities to agree to a new lease to 2007. The next job was to set to work with their family to transform the island, and since 1980 it has been run by Major and Mrs

A Herm mystery. Does this grave contain two victims of cholera or two men drowned after an accident at sea?

Wood's daughter Pennie and son-in-law Adrian Heyworth, the lease now running to 2049.

The Herm of today offers the thriving White House Hotel, which has 40 rooms and a very fine restaurant. There are also a number of self-catering cottages, the Mermaid pub and a campsite. The campsite is so popular with Guernsey people that many of them put their tents up at the start of the summer season and leave them there until the autumn, coming across the short stretch of water just as often as work, school and finances allow.

One feature of the island that offers perfect peace is the little chapel of St Tugual. Regular Sunday morning services are held here for islanders and visitors and are always very welcoming and genuinely moving.

There are even thriving shops in Herm and the Christmas shopping trips from Guernsey are always well supported.

But despite all this what Herm really offers is tranquillity. A half-hour walk from the harbour will either take you around the cliffs or around to the spectacular Shell or Belvoir beaches. In the afternoon, after a light or large lunch, a half-hour walk in the other direction allows you to see the rest of the island.

The cliffs are home to ravens, fulmar petrels and wheatears, and on the common there are flocks of finches, blackbirds, thrushes and of course plenty of rabbits. In early summer puffins nest on the east of the island and on the nearby island of Jethou. They are easy to spot from the cliffs and paths as they wheel and dive in search of sand eels.

The people of Herm – and there are now 55 living here, with 80 more swelling the population during the summer season – are justifiably proud of the island's gardens and wild flowers. A benign micro-climate allows plants to flourish which would not survive just a mile or so away in Guernsey, and in 2002 Herm was a Britain in Bloom Gold Award winner. There is also a vigorous tree-planting policy and 20,000 trees are planted every year.

Herm is a wonderful place to visit in the spring and summer but it is really an island for all seasons. In autumn there are birds to see as they head off on migration, and in winter a day trip to walk the cliffs, enjoy the sounds of the curlews and oystercatchers and sit by the fire in the Mermaid is a perfect way to unwind.

The **harbour** on Herm Island.

Pierre Aux Rats is a column on the common built to replace an earlier menhir.

Fisherman's Cottage is available to let, if you put your name down early enough.

The Harbour Beach. The first of many beaches on Herm.

Shell Beach at low water. This is a favourite spot for Guernsey's nautical daytrippers.

Herm can provide you with a beach all to yourself.

Belvoir Bay is a real suntrap but its deep waters can feel a bit cool to those more used to the Mediterannean.

Passing **Jethou** on the approach to Herm.

The coastal footpath on the east coast.

Opposite page
A fishing boat heading out off **Guernsey** towards Sark with
Jethou in the background.

Alderney

Alderney, the third largest of the Channel Islands and the nearest to the mainland of Britain, lies twenty miles from Guernsey and just eight miles off the Normandy coast. Although only a mile and a half wide and three and a half miles long, it is one of the principal islands of the Bailiwick of Guernsey.

The 2,400-strong population of this little village on a rock enjoys an enviable lifestyle and all the facilities and amenities of a city.

Its airport handles over 80,000 passengers a year arriving by commercial or private aircraft. Braye Harbour, the maritime gateway to the Channel Islands and France, is a popular first port of call, accommodating passenger ferries and freight vessels and welcoming thousands of yachtsmen from all over Europe every year.

The **Alderney Coat of Arms**.

Island life centres around the pretty town of St. Anne, capital of Alderney, with its cobbled streets, colourful cottages, restaurants, pubs, shops and boutiques.

Quality of life matters to the Ridunians (as Alderney people are called) and leisure interests are well catered for. An impressive number of restaurants serve the best of seafood and popular watering holes extend a warm welcome to all visitors.

Alderney's scenic golf course, with stunning panoramic views across Braye Bay and the French coast, is a true challenge even for the most experienced players.

The island offers some of the finest sea fishing in the Channel Islands. Sailing, surfboarding, tennis, squash, badminton, bowls, clay pigeon shooting and cricket are all popular pastimes.

And with over forty clubs and societies ensuring a busy diary of social, cultural and sporting events throughout the year, including the eight-day Alderney Week carnival, there is always something going on.

Alderney is rich in flora and fauna. More than 270 bird species have been logged and among the the wide variety of mammals you'll find bats and blonde hedgehogs! The dramatic coastline embraces wide open commons, sweeping sandy beaches and stunning cliffs and headlands, punctuated with Victorian fortresses and German fortifications.

The island has a fascinating history. Earliest evidence of human habitation is provided by flint tools left by visiting hunter-gatherers, thousands of years ago and other finds prove settlement in Alderney by Bronze and early Iron Age people. The Romans used Alderney as a staging post between Brittany and Britain and the island eventually became part of the Duchy of Normandy and, as such, property of the British Crown.

There followed brief periods of French invasion and looting and stewardship, mainly by the Chamberlain family, until control was vested by the Crown in the Le Mesurier family after the upheavals of the English Civil War.

During the family's 150-year tenure, smuggling, wrecking and wartime privateering brought them and the islanders much wealth. An efficient Militia was established to defend the island and there was much building work carried out to create the 'old harbour' and most of the warehouses at Braye, the old school (now the museum) and almshouses. The Casquets Lighthouse, the 'Island Hall', several extensions to the old parish church and much of the 'Town' were also built during this time.

Smuggling was suppressed by the British government after 1806 and, some time after the Battle of Waterloo, the British garrison was withdrawn and the island fell on hard times. The Crown lands were divided and many families emigrated to Canada, Australia and New Zealand. The population fell to about 1,000.

The present breakwater and the many forts to protect it were constructed between 1847 and 1870 – part of the harbour intended to shelter the entire British Channel fleet to defend Britain against France. A further period of prosperity followed, the imported workers and the garrison bringing the population up to about 7,000 in 1859. However, the 1891 census revealed that after work ceased the population had dropped to 1,857.

The building of these defences, after a visit by Queen Victoria in 1854, initiated the start of Alderney tourism, with visitors anxious to follow in the Queen's footsteps and view the 'government works'. Later, with the continuing rise in tourism, the first airport in the Channel Islands was opened in Alderney in 1936.

By 1939 the permanent population was up to about 2,500, but the war caused the garrison and many local residents to leave and return to England. At the time the island was evacuated in June 1940, ahead of the German advance across Europe, only 1,452 people were left and, except for about a dozen, these were all taken to England and the island virtually abandoned.

A preferred artist's subject especially at sunset. During late spring the **Sister Rocks** are covered by a golden carpet of broom.

From late 1940 the Germans filled the island with slave workers, mainly from eastern Europe, to build part of Hitler's Atlantic Wall, the results of all the concrete they poured still very much in evidence today. This was a particularly grim chapter in Alderney's history.

By the end of the war the island was in such a poor state – mines, fortifications and barbed wire everywhere, many of the houses destroyed by the invaders – that the British government actually considered abandoning it and not allowing the population to return. They later agreed to a limited return and the island to be run as a communal farm for at least two years, the first few islanders arriving back around Christmas 1945.

By 1948 a good number of the pre-war population had returned and a written constitution was agreed with the British government, under which Alderney is still largely governed today. Income and other taxes were instituted for the first time and various services were linked to Guernsey, gradually evolving over the last 55 years to provide education, health and social services, roads and other infrastructure to a standard enjoyed in mainland Britain.

21st-century Alderney

Today the island prides itself on a stable democratic government, the States of Alderney, which consists of the President and ten States Members. In addition, Alderney has two seats with voting rights on the Guernsey States of Deliberation's monthly meetings.

The island's economy is generated from a combination of the traditional industries such as fishing and tourism and, more recently, light industry, consultancies, the financial services sector and in particular e-commerce. Modern telecommunications technology and a computer-literate workforce have pushed Alderney to the forefront of internet-based business communities. Despite its closeness to the mainlands of France and Britain, and a long history of invasions and occupations, Alderney has managed to escape the mass tourism invasion. Many regular visitors who come back year after year – eventually to settle down – hope that Alderney will remain their secret little hideaway for years to come.

Following pages
Fort Clonque

The cobbled **High Street**, with the Alderney Museum, the Coronation Inn, the Campania Inn, the Salvation Army and many colourful and floral cottages, is a busy through road.

The trough in **Marais Square** is a reminder of its past. Once known as La Places des Vaches (Cow Square) the local cattle market took place here. Nowadays there is a small street market on Sundays. But anyone venturing near Marais Square on New Year's Day morning will receive a generous dowsing courtesy of the Alderney Fire Brigade!

Opposite page
St Anne's – one of Alderney's popular and cosy guesthouses. The owner is a particularly keen gardener who scoops annual awards in the Floral Islands of Guernsey competitions.

The bells of **St Anne's**, which ring to announce good, bad or sad news, are favourites among campanologists. During the German Occupation four of the six bells were removed and sent to Cherbourg to be melted down for munitions. After the war they were identified and returned by the garrison engineer and, together with the two remaining bells, were sent to England for re-casting before being re-hung.

The beautiful stained glass windows of **St Anne's Church** portray many different religious scenes as well as island life.

The **Parish Church of St Anne**, also known as 'The Cathedral of the Channel Islands', was built by Sir George Gilbert Scott and consecrated in 1850. St Anne's Church is acknowledged to be one of the finest Victorian buildings in the Channel Islands.

Braye Bay, just a few minutes' walk from town, is one of Alderney's most popular beaches and the venue for a number of annual events such as the New Year's Day swim, the Daft Raft race and the sandcastle competition.

Alderney's scenic but challenging 9-hole golf course offers splendid views over the English Channel and the nearby coast of France. Green fees are the lowest in the Channel Islands.

Run entirely by volunteers of the Alderney Railway Society, and 150 years old in 1997, the **Alderney Railway** is the only working railway in the Channel Islands. Every Saturday and Sunday during the summer season, the diesel engine *Elizabeth* and post-war London Underground carriages take passengers along the 2-mile scenic route from Braye Station to Mannez Quarry.

On the cliff face just below Essex Castle are the dramatic **Hanging Rocks**. These are the subject of numerous legends and known locally as Madame Robilliard's Nose.

Clonque Cottage is one of two small cottages on the track to the Victorian fortress Fort Clonque.

Crabby Harbour, a safe harbour for small local boats, is also the venue for the annual ecumenical Blessing of the Fishing Fleet and the Alderney Week Manpowered Flight competition.

Mannez Lighthouse is now monitored and controlled from the Trinity House Operational Control Centre at Harwich in Essex. Guided tours of the lighthouse are organised during weekends in the main season and by appointment.

The **Gannet Rocks**, among Alderney's most breathtaking sights, are home to one of Europe's largest gannet colonies. Over 7,000 nest here from March to October.

Raz Island and its Victorian fort – past uses for which have included a bird museum and an oyster farm – is in private ownership and linked to Longis Bay by a causeway.

Sark

Sark is an integral part of the Bailiwick of Guernsey but it has a very distinct and separate identity. It regards itself as a feudal fiefdom and, until recently, could fully justify that definition. The history of how Sark came to be part of the Bailiwick of Guernsey is a fascinating one. The island formed a part of the fief of St Ouen in Jersey and was, for a long time, under the control of the de Carteret family.

The island was an adjunct of the Duchy of Normandy and the loyal toast on Sark is still to 'Her Majesty the Queen, the Duke of Normandy.' It was Queen Elizabeth I who first appreciated the importance of the island as a useful haven for supplies and ammunition in the event of conflict with France or Spain.

Helier de Carteret, the seigneur of St Ouen, was summoned to London and given the task of not only inhabiting the island but fortifying it. Her Majesty agreed to his suggestion that the island should be created a fief, which means a piece of land given in exchange for military service.

The de Carteret family eventually lost its control of Sark when Sir Philippe de Carteret backed the losing side in the English Civil War. Jersey sometimes thinks of Sark as the island that got away.

The history of Sark involves shifting allegiances, French and German occupation and, now, external pressures coming to bear which are threatening to end something unique in western civilisation.

The German Occupation in 1940 was a defining moment for Sark, as it was for the rest of the Channel Islands. At that time the seigneur of Sark was Sybil Hathaway, a woman for whom the word indomitable could have been coined.

Under her firm and principled leadership the people of Sark mostly stayed in place when the invasion forces landed and tried to keep their very individual way of living as intact as possible despite the aliens in their midst.

During the occupation Mrs Hathaway, the legendary Dame of Sark, proved to be a formidable opponent to the Germans and when liberation came she firmly took control again and supervised the surrender of the occupying forces.

Over the years Sark has made its living from silver mining, fishing and agriculture. The island is now home to 600 people and depends, essentially, on tourism. There are a number of wealthy residents who live from investment and business, and a thriving involvement in providing offshore services for the finance industry grew and flourished during the 1980s. Much of the recent development and modernisation of the island has been paid for by money made supporting the finance industry.

The only way to get to Sark is by sea. The ferry trip from Guernsey takes 40 minutes and the arrival at Maseline Harbour is truly impressive, the cliffs towering over the harbour and a spectacular white lighthouse looming high on the cliff top.

Then the only way is up. A ten-minute walk to ascend the very steep Harbour Hill can be avoided by taking a ride on the tractor-pulled 'toast rack'. Unless you are infirm it seems a shame to miss the climb, the rewards for which in early summer are spectacular displays of wild flowers.

The first thing to greet you at the top is the very welcome sight of the Bel Air pub – and the realisation that there are no cars on Sark. Transport is by foot, bicycle or horsedrawn carriage. The tractors are supposed to be for agricultural purposes but the practical people of Sark appreciate that they are very useful for going to the shops for the groceries.

The best way to get around is either on foot or a bike. Bike riding is big in Sark. Watching the guests arrive at a Sark wedding is quite a sight as the very smartly dressed ladies try to keep their hats on as they cycle to church.

The main street of Sark is an amalgam of flimsy wood and metal constructions and some very smart granite buildings. There is a Wild West look to the main street and on a windy day it would not be surprising to see tumbleweed rolling down the road towards you.

Sark is really a plateau that looks something like the top of a South Wales mountain but surrounded by blue sea and not green valleys. It is great walking country and it is small enough to get right around in a day.

Although Sark is small it is, amazingly, two islands. The smaller island, Little Sark, is connected to its big brother by a causeway called La Coupee. This is more than 200 feet high and on a day when the wind blows hard it can present a considerable challenge to the more nervous who try to cross it – but in any weather the crossing is well worth making. Little Sark is yet another world.

Sark has plenty to entertain visitors. The cliffs on the west coast are in some years home to peregrine falcons, and watching them wheeling through the sky in pursuit of pigeons is worth the boat fare in itself.

And if you are prepared to tackle the walk down and, more significantly, the climb back up, there are superb beaches waiting for you.

Then there is food. Sark is well blessed with

hotels and restaurants. A Sark lobster lunch with a good bottle of chilled Chablis remains the defining memory of many international bankers and businessmen who have travelled to the island for board meetings.

Modern Sark is having to face up to change. European legislation, the European Court of Human Rights and the British government are not comfortable with an independently-minded people who have evolved a way of life that has worked with considerable success for many generations but has paid little attention to politically correct mores.

The changes are coming. The island needs new sources of revenue to fund its school, health facilities and other social amenities. A new system of taxation will soon be introduced to tax people who had previously managed to get by with taxation that was more voluntary than compulsory.

The old feudal traditions may soon vanish under the juggernaut of European demands. Already the island parliament, Chief Pleas, is having to transform itself from a body that comprised the major landowners and some elected officials to something that is more acceptable to the modern European model.

Some of these changes may be for the good but they risk destroying a way of life that has suited the local people for many generations and has offered no threat to anyone outside the island. The people of Sark are wonderfully welcoming to those who come to visit them and share the delights of their island. They are not so keen on people who abuse the hospitality of the place. For them, a night in the smallest jail in Britain or a speedy trip back to the boat remain the most likely options.

Whatever happens to Sark during the upheavals of the first years of the 21st century, it must be hoped that the tranquillity of this idyllic place will not be too badly affected.

It is on a day when no boats have come in that the unique island atmosphere becomes most apparent. When the only people around are locals and those visitors staying on the island, the magical qualities of this little rock in the ocean focus mind and spirit on the fact that on such a day as this, the rest of the world is cut off from the extraordinary island of Sark – and it doesn't know what it's missing.

The lighthouse at **Port Robert** dominates Maseline Harbour in Sark.

When in **Sark** take to the bicycle.

La Seigneurie gardens are amongst Sark's most visited attractions.

St Peter's Church. Please park your bicycles on the right.

Following pages The eye of the needle on Sark's west cliffs with **Brecqhou** in the distance.

The old boys' school.

Even the post office is pretty in Sark.

Opposite page
Sark's alternative transport.

Looking north from Sark's west coast. Peregrine falcons have been seen nesting near here.

The tiny **Creux Harbour**. Alderney's massive harbour was built in Victorian times to hold the entire Channel fleet. Cynical fishermen say that the present day Channel fleet could now be housed in Creux.

La Coupee connects Big and Little Sark. This is where you have to get off your bicycle to make the crossing.

Sark's beaches are a long way down.

A hidden gem in **Little Sark**.

Let the horse take the strain. The traditional way to get around.

Guernsey: beyond there is America. Looking westward out towards the Atlantic.